When the Un*every*thing_{able} Happened

by Lorraine de Kleuver

www.alysbooks.com

To Rosalie Violet

The Adventures of Felix and Pip – When the Uneverythingable Happened
Copyright © Lorraine de Kleuver
Illustration copyright © Lorraine de Kleuver

First Edition 2018
Published by Aly's Books

www.alysbooks.com
Your Book | Our Mission

Designed by Fish Biscuit
fishbiscuitdesign.com.au

All rights reserved. No part of this book may be reproduced or transmitted in any form or by any means, electronic, mechanical, photocopying or otherwise without the prior permission of the publisher.

ISBN: 978-0-6480017-9-9

High up in the sky over Williamstown, two young seagulls were flying towards the ship called 'The Castlemaine'.

The two young seagulls were the best of friends. They were always seen flying around together, and the only way their mates could tell them apart, was that Chips had a purple birthmark on his left foot. Both were nicknamed after the food they loved most, and Potato Cake loved eating potato cake leftovers from the ground.

"How about we land on the tall radar pole on 'The Castlemaine'?" called out Potato Cake to Chips.

"I'm almost there," Chips called back.

When they landed and settled onto the radar pole, they both looked down below to watch a boat moor up against Gem Pier.

The boat was manned by two animals. As the larger one turned the big wheel to bring the boat closer to the pier, the smaller one jumped onto the pier with a rope in its hands.

The boat was a catamaran called Purr-fect, and the two animals sailing on her were called Felix and Pip.

They watched the fluffy dog and the little water rat moor up to Gem Pier.

"Wow, those two animals look like they're having fun," Chips said.

"Yeah, but not as much fun as we have when we're racing each other," replied Potato Cake.

After they both caught their breath, Chips challenged Potato Cake to another race.

"Let's race to the rotunda at the park over there."

"Okay," agreed Potato Cake.

As the two seagulls positioned themselves, Potato Cake called the count. "One. . . Two. . . Three!"

Off they flew at speed to the red-roofed rotunda.

While Potato Cake and Chips were flying as fast as they could, Felix and Pip left Purr-fect to take a walk into town.

"I would just love a banana ice cream," said Pip eagerly, as they walked along the pier.

"I'm hungry too, but I'd prefer a yummy vanilla ice cream. . . sooo creamy."

They laughed and enjoyed the sunny day, thinking about sitting down on the grass with their ice creams.

In the meantime, Potato Cake and Chips had landed on top of the red roof of the rotunda.

"I beat you again," Potato Cake boasted.

As chips tried to catch his breath, he managed to spurt out, "Yeah, but you flew off on the count of two." He grumbled and waved his right wing at Potato Cake. He was unhappy.

As the two seagulls grizzled back and forth, Felix and Pip were coming closer to the shops.

"Um, I can smell the most wonderful smell of fish 'n' chips," Pip said. She lifted her nose in the direction of the aroma.

"Oh yesss," a hungry Felix replied. "I think I'll change my mind on the ice cream and have fish 'n' chips instead."

Back on the roof of the rotunda, Potato Cake fessed up. He admitted that he got a little excited and perhaps flew off earlier than he should have. "I'm sorry," he said. "How about another race? You can do the counting."

"Okay, that sounds fair." Chips flapped out his wings, ready to take his position for the next race. "How about we race to that red fountain over there?"

"No probs." Potato Cake drew in a deep breath.

Chips started the count again. "One... Two... Three!"

With determination, they both raced off.

Although Potato Cake was a little heavier than Chips, he was also a little stronger. He often outpaced Chips. But Chips was determined to win this race.

Chips was trying his best to keep ahead of Potato Cake. He flapped and flapped his wings, but Potato Cake was gaining.

Chips began to get puffed out and grabbed a water bottle that had been left on a table. The couple of seconds he took to take a few sips of water, cost him precious time. Potato Cake flew past him.

Chips' heart sank.

Across the road from the park, a large dog sat watching the two seagulls race each other. The dog was called Simba. His massive body took up most of the path.

A young lady walked past Simba. She kept her little dog close by, afraid that Simba would eat her little doggy up. But Simba didn't. He just sat there quietly, watching everyone.

As Potato Cake and Chips were nearing the red fountain, Simba yawned. When he opened his mouth wide, everyone could see his many sharp teeth.

When a little girl was about to cross the road, she saw Simba's mighty yawn, and she dropped her ice cream in fright.

"Mummy, Mummy," she cried. "Look. A big, big dog is going to eat us."

At the same time, Potato Cake was flying over the little girl. He saw her ice-cream fall to the ground. For a split second Potato Cake took his eye off the fountain, and what happened next was... unthinkable... unbelievable... unimaginable... it was... uneverythingable!

Chips, who was seconds behind Potato Cake, yelled, "Watch out." But, it was too late. Potato Cake had crashed right into the red water fountain.

His feathers were everywhere!

All the seagulls in the area flew to the fountain. They were squawking loudly and picking at Potato Cake's feathers, trying to pull him out. All poor Chips could do was try to comfort his friend.

"You'll be alright. Try not to panic. We'll get you out. Don't worry." Chips tried everything to calm his friend down.

Hearing all the commotion Felix and Pip left their fish 'n' chips on a bench seat, and ran around to the red fountain. There were feathers everywhere, and seagulls calling out, "Help, help, we need help here."

Felix ran quickly up a tall flower stem to get a better view of what was happening. "It looks like a seagull has got stuck in the wrought iron work of the fountain," Felix told Pip.

Pip stretched to her full height as she leaned up against the fountain. She urged Felix to climb on her back and jump inside. Felix scampered up to where he could see the injured seagull.

"Oh my," he gasped when he saw the seagull was in trouble. Potato Cake's head and beak were stuck.

Felix knew that this seagull needed help fast. Before scurrying back to Pip, he tried to reassure the seagull that he was getting help. But Potato Cake was quickly getting tired, flapping his wings to keep himself up.

While Felix considered how best to free Potato Cake, all the seagulls kept calling out.

"Please try and help him."

"How bad is he?"

"He can't last like this. His wings will give up."

Chips got close enough to speak to Felix directly. "While you and your friend get help. We'll try and support his body."

Time was of the essence.

Felix called down to Pip "We need something big and strong to be able to reach Potato Cake."

"He's in a bad way. You need to hurry Pip."

"I'm right on it," she called back.

As she turned to climb down from the water fountain, Pip couldn't believe her eyes. There in front of her was the largest dog she had ever seen. Its head was almost the size of her body. She froze, too scared to do anything.

"Hello, I'm Simba," the giant dog said. "I was across the road and saw what happened. Can I help you?"

Pip couldn't believe their luck. She turned to Felix, "We're so lucky Felix, this is Simba," she introduced Simba to him.

Felix climbed down towards where Pip was pointing. "Oh my gosh," he stammered. "No offense Simba, but you are massive."

"No offense taken," Simba replied.

"I'm Felix, and this is my friend, Pip. Are we glad to see YOU."

Simba walked around to where Potato Cake was stuck. He stood high up on his hind legs and used a paw to support Potato Cake's exhausted body. Tears of relief flowed from Potato Cake's eyes when he realised this massive dog was there to save him.

Felix and Pip positioned themselves next to Potato Cake. Simba carefully and gently slid one paw around Potato Cake's body, whilst supporting his weight with the other.

Once he felt Potato Cake was secure, Simba told Felix and Pip that if they pushed Potato Cake's beak out towards him, he would be able to pull Potato Cake out.

On the count of three, they freed Potato Cake together.

Felix, Pip and Chips, and all the other seagulls raced to Simba. Simba held Potato Cake gently in his paw. Potato Cake seemed lifeless. Chips stroked his friend and started to cry.

"Don't worry little buddy, your friend is okay. He's just exhausted. We need to let him rest," Simba reassured him.

Everyone gathered around Simba, where Potato Cake rested on Simba's large paw. Potato Cake's beak was very bruised and damaged.

Simba walked over to a more protected area and laid Potato Cake carefully on some lush green grass.

Felix insisted, "We must try and protect his beak with a bandage."

Chips addressed his fellow seagulls, "Who would like to donate a feather to make a bandage for Potato Cake?"

Without thinking they each plucked out one of their own feathers and queued up, ready to pass their feather on to Felix.

With Pip holding Potato Cake's head in his paw, Felix was able to collect and wrap all the donated feathers. He fastened them all with a soft stem from a plant nearby.

When Felix was happy with Potato Cake's feather bandage, Pip lowered his head onto a feather pillow.

In the meantime, Simba went around the park with all the seagulls and collected some tree branches to build a fire to keep Potato Cake warm.

Once the fire started to crackle, they all gathered around Potato Cake to keep him company and watch over him. Potato Cake slept quietly as night fell.

As the first rays of morning sun pierced through the trees and onto the park, Potato Cake began to wake up. Chips woke to his friend's stirring.

When Potato Cake opened his eyes, he sat bolt upright. He grabbed at his beak, trying to tear away his bandage. With garbled-like sounds, he tried to call for help.

Quickly, Chips grabbed his wings to stop him from pulling off his bandage. "Stop, Stop," Chips cried out to his friend.

Within moments, everyone was at Potato Cake's side. They all gently assured him that the bandage was to protect his beak and reminded him of his terrible accident.

Chips placed both of his wings on his friend's shoulders and murmered, "You must keep your bandage on. Your beak is badly bruised and injured, and I bet it is very sore."

Potato Cake nodded in agreement.

"You'll be okay. Our new friends have made sure that your beak will heal well."

Potato Cake looked around at everyone that helped to save him. He tried to say thank you, but his words sounded funny.

Chips gave his friend a hug and walked him over to all his new friends.

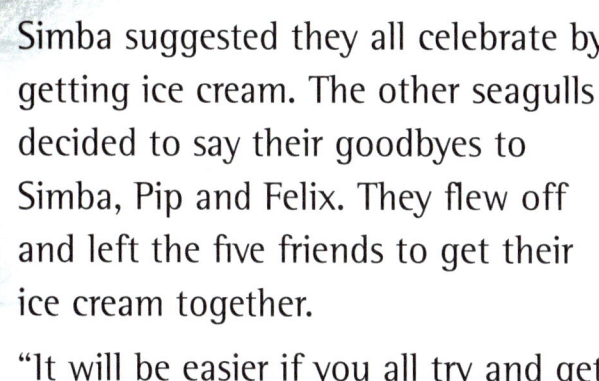

Simba suggested they all celebrate by getting ice cream. The other seagulls decided to say their goodbyes to Simba, Pip and Felix. They flew off and left the five friends to get their ice cream together.

"It will be easier if you all try and get onto my back," offered Simba.

Within an instant, the two seagulls flew onto his shoulders. Felix and Pip jumped onto his back too.

"All comfortable?" asked Simba.

"Yes," they all replied.

"Well then," Simba exclaimed. "Let's go and find us an ice-cream shop."

The five friends soon found what they were after. The Ice Cream Shoppe sold all sorts of ice cream—even doggy ice cream.

"Yippie," they all called out.

After a few days, Potato Cake's beak was beginning to heal. Simba, Pip and Felix decided that it was time for them to return home.

In that time, they all had become the best of friends, and on parting, promised each other to meet up sometime.

As boat Purr-fect pulled away from Gem Pier, they all waved goodbye to each other.

As the two seagulls flew over the pier, they called out, "We will never forget the help you gave us."

And with that, Felix and Pip sailed Purr-fect back home to Werribee South.

Author's Notes

'Uneverythingable'

While writing this story, of Potato Cake crashing into the water fountain, I was trying to think hard of a word that would best describe this disastrous event. As you can see in the story I was using words that began with 'un'.

This (un) is called a 'prefix.'

When you're at school, around grades three, four and five, you will learn more about prefixes, and whole lot of other stuff about words – so I'll leave it up to your teachers, to teach you.

However, using the prefix 'un' was important because I wanted 'my' word to sound really bad – and I mean the worst of the worst accidents to happen. In my frustration in trying to find a really bad word, I decided to collect some of the 'un' words that I knew and put them altogether as one big bad word – and UNEVERYTHINGABLE was born.

So when you want to best describe a really bad accident, like what happened to Potato Cake – then 'Uneverythingable' is the best!

Try saying it with your eyes wide open, your mouth really, really wide open, both hands up in the air, then slapping them down on your knees – in a real 'Oh My Gosh' moment.

You'll agree with me, it's the best 'un' really, really bad word!

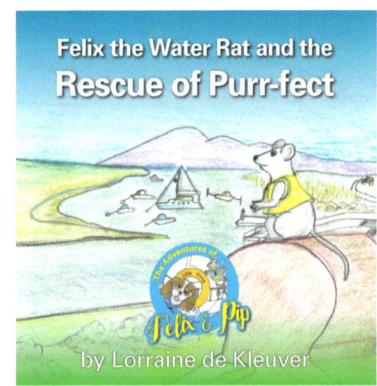
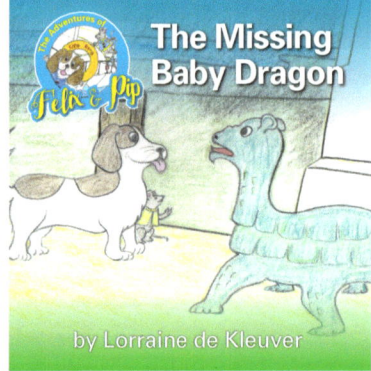
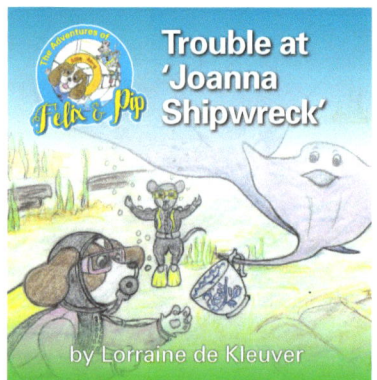

www.ingramcontent.com/pod-product-compliance
Lightning Source LLC
Chambersburg PA
CBHW042144290426
44110CB00002B/112